JOURNEYWOMAN

Copyright © 2017 Carolyne Van Der Meer

Except for the use of short passages for review purposes, no part of this book may be reproduced, in part or in whole, or transmitted in any form or by any means, electronically or mechanically, including photocopying, recording, or any information or storage retrieval system, without prior permission in writing from the publisher.

Canada Council for the Arts / Conseil des Arts du Canada

ONTARIO ARTS COUNCIL
CONSEIL DES ARTS DE L'ONTARIO
an Ontario government agency
un organisme du gouvernement de l'Ontario

Canada

The publisher gratefully acknowledges the support of the Canada Council for the Arts and the Ontario Arts Council for its publishing program. The publisher is also grateful for the financial assistance received from the Government of Canada.

Front cover artwork: Ariane Côté, "Journeywoman," oil and resin on plexiglass, 24 x 36 inches, 2017. Website: arianecote.com.

Cover design: Val Fullard

Library and Archives Canada Cataloguing in Publication

Van Der Meer, Carolyne A., 1968–, author
    Journeywoman / poems by Carolyne Van Der Meer.

(Inanna poetry and fiction series)
Poems.
Issued in print and electronic formats.
ISBN 978-1-77133-449-5 (softcover).-- ISBN 978-1-77133-450-1 (epub).--
ISBN 978-1-77133-451-8 (Kindle).-- ISBN 978-1-77133-452-5 (pdf)

    I. Title. II. Series: Inanna poetry and fiction series

PS8643.A5265J68 2017   C811'.6   C2017-905459-7
                                            C2017-905460-0

Printed and bound in Canada

Inanna Publications and Education Inc.
210 Founders College, York University
4700 Keele Street, Toronto, Ontario M3J 1P3 Canada
Telephone: (416) 736-5356   Fax (416) 736-5765
Email: inanna.publications@inanna.ca
Website: www.inanna.ca

FSC
www.fsc.org

MIX
Paper from
responsible sources
FSC® C004071

JOURNEYWOMAN

POEMS BY

Carolyne Van Der Meer

Inanna poetry & fiction series

INANNA Publications and Education Inc.
Toronto, Canada

For my sister, Alicia, the real journeywoman

Contents

Preface   xi

I: MANOEUVRING

(S)mothering	3
Running at The 'Y'	5
Breaking Glass at Karen's	6
Folding the Sheets	9
I Will Long for This	10
The Sewing Box	11
Where Is My Off Button?	13
Buoy on the St. Lawrence	14
Windows	18
Lesson at Masala Cooking School	19
Mowing the Lawn in Lacey Green	20
The Reconstruction	21
Homemade Pasta on New Year's Eve	23
Teatotaler	24
In the Dental Chair	26
Magnetic Resonance	28

II: TRAVELOGUE

Atonement	33
Busking on Shop Street with Oscar Wilde	34
Private Meeting with Oscar Wilde	35
At Jim Morrison's Grave, Père Lachaise, Paris	36

From Bog Bodies to Thinking Men	37
Visiting Yeats at Thoor Ballylee	38
All Hallow's Eve	39
Sizing Up Patrick in County Down	40
St. Laurence O'Toole Unbarred	41
Passages	42
Wind, Sand and Stars on Highway 401	44
Puppy Fat at the Rijksmuseum	46
The List	47
Finding the Hollandsche Schouwberg	49
Buying Sandals in Oltrarno	51
Leather Shop in the Via Francesco Crispi	53
Re-imagining Italy on the Train	54
Writing Verse by the Palacio Real	56
Tapas in the Plaza Ana	58
Barcelona Beach	59

III: THE CANCER JOURNEY

ABVD	63
Hodgkin's Dreamscape	66
Clinical Trial	67
Fear of Relapse	68
His Name Was Lefty	69
Sensory Memory	70

IV: FELLOW TRAVELLERS

Emily's Moorland Ghost	73
Meeting Saint Agnes in the Piazza Navona	74

The Philosophy of Hijab	76
Prayer on a Train	78
Newtown Abbey, Trim	80
At the Tennis Club	82
Reunion	84
The Vocation of Jeanne Le Ber	86
Acknowledgements	90

Preface

Ralph Waldo Emerson said that "Life is a journey, not a destination." But it's much more complex than this, isn't it?

The word "journeyman" refers to an individual who has completed an apprenticeship and has been fully trained in a trade—but who is not yet a master. What does it take to become a master? Why, the journey, of course.

The *Online Etymology Dictionary* tells us that journey, from circa 1200, is "a defined course of travelling; one's path in life"; from Old French *journée*, a "day's work or travel"; from Vulgar Latin *diurnum* "day," the noun use of neuter of Latin *diurnus* "of one day." The meaning an "act of travelling by land or sea" is from circa 1300. In Middle English it also meant "a day" (circa 1400); a day's work (mid-fourteenth century); "distance travelled in one day" (mid-thirteenth century), and as recently as Johnson (1755), the primary sense was still "the travel of a day." In the mid-fourteenth century, the meaning evolved to "travel[ling] from one place to another," from the Anglo-French *journeyer*, from the Old French *journoiier* "work by day; go, walk, travel," and from *journée*, "a day's work or travel."

My notion of "journeywoman" is a mix of these things. It is really about the journey a woman makes—not just towards being an apprentice and then a master of all that womanhood offers, but also, the physical journey. Where does life take us? Through girlhood, womanhood, motherhood and beyond. The waif, the mother, and the crone—and the phases that make up each stage—these are what make us first apprentices and then master craftswomen. To get there, we make many journeys.

And so we are journeywomen.

I.
Manoeuvring

(S)mothering

I can be no one else
when my mother is with me

> *You might have been difficult sometimes*
> *but you weren't a brat,* she says.
> *I put all my energy into you.*
> *I thought of you as my shadow.*
>
> *What? In that I was always with you?*
> *or that I was like you?*
>
> *A bit of both.*

The critical eye
I imagine watching me
as I mother my own child
seems not so critical.
Briefly, I see her differently.

So who is real?
the ones we are,
have created,
the ones who reappear?

I consider my own mothering
as I coax my son to lie down.
Do-do, I say. *Sleep.*
Gentle, liquid eyes, round,
he falls to his knees,

pulls himself into the fetal position,
curls his hands into his chest,
like me. I soothe him,
he is the one person
who is calmed by me,
is where
I put my energy.

Running at the "Y"

My legs ripple with muscle
reflect in the dark windows
yes, this is good
Is muscle all I want?
No. I want a small ass

I watch the other runners
feel the charge of competition
want to be faster
thinner
younger

Indentations
in my buttocks
absorbing the shock of each stride
searing into me
like the exhausting, exhilarating wrench
of childbirth
or after intense
sex
like your loins will fall from you

I'll take the smaller ass
but not
in exchange for
motherhood

Breaking Glass at Karen's

I'm standing at the kitchen counter
toying with the smooth
surface of my wine glass
Laughter, eyes meet and
wink, conversation flows
Fingers catch the base
before I can wrap them around
the stem, the ding of crystal on
granite, the gushing of red liquid
everywhere, in jars, on plates,
all the places it should not be

At Jewish weddings
goblet under
the groom's right foot,
he presses down
it splinters

I'm amazed the glass
remains unbroken,
panic to mop up
the burgundy as it seeps
into every crack
and crevice
runs down the side
of the island
threatening to stain
elegant clothes

guests back away
in caution

Not even an hour later, as I lift my
hand to brush my husband's shoulder, it
catches his empty glass
bounces on the granite
I catch it before it hits again,
its life prolonged, no liquid lost—
my face and neck red hot with
embarrassment, choked laughter in my
throat as Karen wraps her arms
round my shoulders

After the breaking of the glass
the bride and groom consider
this lifetime of trust
the breaking
of one thing leading to
the fusion of another

The evening draws to a close, I sip water, set
the tumbler down hard
it shatters,
slivers catch the light
We laugh, clean up with moistened towels

Karen remembers a story

how the glass
represents
the looking glass
reflecting the shift
we sometimes make
without knowing

Folding the Sheets

You take your end
two corners
blue diamonds, white linen
I take mine
We step towards each other
four corners meet
fingers touch
I let go, walk back
My fingers gliding along the
smooth edges
pick up the end of
the half, we can't decide
whether to halve it

the long way or the short
laugh, go short
years later
see our friendship
broken
but still
I walk to you
two-step
trust in your
cakewalk to
halve it again
fold it crisply

into a perfect square

I Will Long for This

I will long for it
the smell of must in your hair from sweat and sleep,
the moulding of your scrawny body into mine
as we sit on a fading porch chair early,
sun barely awake
You come to say good morning,
mumble I love you,
grains of sleep in your eyes,
fold backward, into me,
I take your small hand
want to hold tight
but you squirm
then scurry to watch cartoons

The Sewing Box

She has put it off for weeks, replacing the broken button on his jacket cuff
because of the full-to-the-brim vintage sewing box
and the *à la carte* bag of spare buttons and thread filaments
that have accumulated through a history of purchases

Cup of Earl Grey by her side, she finally looks in the box
a wooden accordion contraption that anyone who sews
would recognize, its tiered compartments only visible
upon lifting the twin lids and pulling them outward

Random pins and bits of tangled thread fill the slotted chambers
cards sporting extra buttons, some with fancy designer names, others not
lists of materials—100% cotton; 80% rayon, 20% nylon;
70% mohair, 30% acrylic; the indisputable 100% pure virgin wool

These breakdowns, no matter how predictable
never fail to hold her attention through the fine print as she opens
the pin tin, sorts those with coloured heads from those without
into their destinations, where you could indeed hear the pin drop

And the Kraft peanut butter jar a pudgy bear
that holds the old button collection, ones from her own small years
from which she fishes out a long ribbon of favourites
strung together by her son when he was little enough to care

military buttons, those covered in silk or flecked with gold
ones shaped like anchors, others like suns
still others with their brand stamped in thin, fine lettering—
she holds it up, this necklace of jewels, smiles, and having failed

to locate the match for the suit cuff, lowers it back into the jar,
separates iron-on tape and stretches of lace, suede elbow patches,
needle threaders with their Queen Wilhelmina faces, snipped ends from
too-long trousers, sewing machine bobbins for multi-coloured strands

Making a pile of refuse and rejects, fingers the specimens she keeps
sometimes cutting them from cardboard labels or old tags deep in the
à la carte bag, sees in them a map of choices, the wheat from chaff
the fork in the proverbial road

Some hours later when she settles on the missing button
she notes it's not a perfect match, stitches it into place
careful to slip it partially under another button in the row of four
just like the tailors do—and seeks her husband's approval

He nods, says quietly *no one will notice*
slips his hand into hers, where, despite the years
it doesn't quite fit, and under her breath
she says, *no one will notice*
squeezes hard

Where Is My Off Button?

It's what he asks in the half-light
laughing with giddy delight at his
cleverness. The glare from the street casts a
bar across his face, the devilish grin

fragmented, one eye dancing
Find it, mommy! he challenges me,
Can you find it, please? My fingers slip across
his small body, hesitating over his belly, stopping

on the knot of his navel. *No, that's my on button!*
he giggles. My own laughter falls in sync
as I resort to tickling. *Stop, stop!* he shrieks, rolling
away. *Hold me, mommy, just hold me*

suddenly calming. The twilight air catches me
in the dog days of summer
just hours after cheering through a baseball game,
the magic of the day climaxing in nightfall

I'm scared, he says.
I hold him. *Everything is fine*, I say.
We are both here, daddy and I
there is nothing to be afraid of,

stroke his hair. *What can I think about?* he asks, willing
a good dream on his journey towards sleep. I rhyme off a list,
watching his eyes widen, and his mouth form *oh yes*
as though he had forgotten the endless possibilities for happiness.

Buoy on the St. Lawrence

Every July we'd pack the car
drive the 20 minutes
to Rivercrest on Highway 2, take the winding
road through dense forest
honking the horn as we rounded corners
to warn of our passage
We'd reach the cottage
square box with
wooden shutters that we'd hoist up
air out the place
Large sunroom parlour overlooking the river
squares of rattan carpet and wicker chairs
cushioned two-seaters, glass table tops
old movie magazines I flipped through
looking for but never finding Shaun Cassidy and Parker Stevenson
Above it, a huge bedroom, same shuttered windows
at least three beds
where my sister and friend
of the summer would stay

We were nestled in community
other cottages, white siding, green
shutters, New England feel
I remember the names on walkway plaques
The Annex, The Lintons, The Richards—
a clan, owned a cluster of six
just beside ours
But it wasn't ours
rather the unused and valuable

real estate of Mr. Burns
my mother's immigration sponsor from the 50s
gave her the keys after his
wife died, said *Here, use it*
He never joined us
never checked up

We weren't good enough
for the Richards
They remembered my
mother as the Burns' nanny
watching over rich James' kids
swimming with James Jr., little Eleanor
down from The Point
the limestone tip of the cottage cluster
where everyone dove in
let the current carry them to
their dwellings downstream
remembering
that years before
my mother was hired help
We swam The Point
caught perch and bass, cleaned them,
got scales in our hair

We were removed
those summers
from our lives on Boundary Road
the little bungalow on the same street

as the city dump
We didn't want
to be associated with the likes of Fred
MacCrae, who horked in my sister's
hair as she got on the bus

We visited the "sweetheart tree"
in the woods behind
the cottages, ran our fingers
along the rough carvings
of hearts, arrows, initials
done by young men
or their lovestruck girlfriends
before they went off to Dieppe or liberated Holland
wondered who they were, what lives they had led

We'd wait for the ocean liners
to sail upstream against
the St. Lawrence current
watch the red and white buoys
bob violently as the vessels
worked their way west
We'd feel the cottage walls shake and
yell *Let's go!*
Even after dark
race
to pull
on trunks
speed down the stairs
out the door to the wharf, jump in
our tiny bay, filled with moss-covered
boulders, wait for ships to

suck water out as they fought the
current, get pulled out
thrown back
pummelled, landing hard in the wet
never thinking we could
smash against the rocks
laughing deep, belly laughs
My mother crazy to let us do it
but in that instant
there was no Boundary Road
no MacCraes
just us
rising naturally
with the crashing waves

Windows

There are men in my house today
unloading glass panes and aluminum
frames, ladders, saws, crowbars
lime-coloured insulation,
noxious spray that makes new windows

glide with ease
The men, they do not
glide but stomp
push

force and grunt
old windows out
push new ones in

surround them with pristine
frames, white
glistening
Someone recently told me
women use 10,000 words a day
Men use only half

These men use
no words
take their noise,
leave a sparkling
clarity of view
echo of unsaid

Lesson at Masala Cooking School

Point Saint-Charles, Montreal

Spoon the spices
on a white plate,
see them side by side.
No scooping and
dumping willy nilly,
says Ilyas, his heavy-lidded eyes
caressing innuendo.
He forces the powders
into thin lines
great staunches of vibrant colour—
red chestnut cayenne,
coriander the shade of gritty sand,
a filament of ochre turmeric.
We hear the clink
of stainless steel spoon
on porcelain, watch the colours
shimmy down a horizontal
plane into the bowl.
Later, as I taste the butter chicken
I swear
he snake-charmed those spices
into a sensual medley.
When he asks me for the fee
again, I remind him I have
already paid. He laughs, says
I was just looking for a way
to keep you here.

Mowing the Lawn in Lacey Green

She braces herself
against the violent
recoil of the engine crank,
against noise
with a garden-gloved hand,
holds down the lever
to engage the motor
and yanks
It stutters,
hangs on, sends a jolt
through her body
as it gains momentum
Back on her haunches
in steel-toed boots,
she begins her slow waltz
with the machine,
moving diagonally across the lawn,
starts in the middle and moves
outwards, the distance
shorter with each return

She looks back at the random pattern,
refuses to read her fortune
in the haphazard clusters
of mown grass
strewn in her wake

The Reconstruction

She is dangerous with knives,
wielding every wrong done
in the whip hand of slicing
crusty bread,
stinging onions, acidic tomatoes,
bound up
in one swipe of blade

The tears squeeze out—
even the onions
have it in for her
She brings up the blade
in an act of self-defence,
forgetting where the tips
of the fingers on her holding hand
are positioned

She lets the steel fall,
everything slows
in surreal crimson
as she sees fleshy tips
among the onion skin
now she knows what it's like
to inflict pain
be at fault
to do it without thinking
to be inflictor
the afflicted

She scoops
the bloody molten ends,
presses them against
her saddened digits,
surrounds them with ice—
gingerly calls an ambulance
and waits, ready
to be reconstructed

Homemade Pasta on New Year's Eve

Suburban Montreal

I watch him as he massages the flour and eggs
Eating is sensual, preparation too
The more you put into it, the better it tastes,
he whispers, tongue
caressing each word

His biceps flex quietly
as I wrap around him from behind
press into his backside, fingers encircling
his arms as he rhythmically kneads

We slice the dough
stretch pieces through the pasta maker
watch as the linguini grows
slide the noodles into boiling water

Later when I roll them around my fork
with porcini mushrooms drenched in cream
I savour the harmony of tastes
remember the hardness
his arms

shudder, satiated, understand
the more you put into it

Teatotaler

She accepts the offer of a rich chai
from her sister-in-law
who stirs scents of coriander and cardamom
sets the cup down
in a gesture of familial affection

They come into her office
at intervals
knowing there is an open invitation
the containers of loose-leaf tea
on the filing cabinet
a comfort she provides without conditions

Now and again she asks him
dear friend to pick up
a box of Barry's
her favourite Assam blend
wrap it in brown paper
send it overseas
he does

Her husband makes her orange pekoe
squeezes a dollop of honey in the cup
comments that even their teabags
share relations
always leaving the tin together

She fingers the porcelain filigree
brings the gold gilt to her lips
all these essences
in one slow sip

In the Dental Chair

Gum Graft Surgery in Ste-Geneviève, Quebec

She tries not to look
at her reflection in their glasses
as they drill, dig, poke
make room for tissue
to save her teeth

She imagines tiny
pink shovelfuls
on the sterile cloth
building on the bone
as they stop to refreeze her
over and over
cover her with a blanket
soak up
adrenaline and sweat
stop her from jumping
at each vibration
metal against flesh
while tears stream
from a frozen eye

When they are done
she drools cries
tries to speak

slurs words makes no
sense sees in the mirror
facial muscles that
drop pull down

In Byzantine times, there was a fine line
between the village idiot the village savant
Today she knows
the difference

Magnetic Resonance

Earplugs, headphones, hairnet in place, perfectly still in the magnetic field
where the pulsing and gyrating of the machine envelopes me but
to my surprise I am soon at ease in this temporary state of imposed paralysis

where in this donut of excited hydrogen atoms, the radio frequency signal is measured in tesla
but its inventor Nikola and I are not on speaking terms—his is a language I don't quite get
so I calibrate to another rhythm, imagining horses galloping

poems writing themselves as I sink into a secondary consciousness
The classical music the erratic webers of magnetic flux density the distant voice
of the technician all serve to soothe me as I feel the twitches of sleep lap at the edges

of my world. I float in and out of worry over brief shudders, momentary
knee jerks, my fingers, my epiglottis. The more I tell myself not to swallow the more
I fear choking. The more I clench my joints into disuse the more they clatter

into agitation. And then, unexpectedly, the cacophony of pounding hooves
the swirling of unwritten poems the mellifluousness of viola strings the stranger's voice

blend into a symphony and I sleep until the atoms return to an
 equilibrium state.

And when I wake, I feel I have travelled so far, resolved much
and deserved the reprieve—though the doctor may read it
 differently.

II.
Travelogue

Atonement

Near Dublin, Ireland

By Mullingar, we were through the worst of it,
the rain pelting on the windshield,
its relentlessness
an argument
that had no beginning no end
just turned 'round us again and again
I could feel your gaze
moving from my face
to the road ahead
back again, waiting
for the answer I refused
to give
What did I want,
your words
lost
in the telling rhythm
of those furious wipers—
On the roundabout, the rain
now a drizzle,
you took the exit for Athlone
before I could tell you
where to go

Busking on Shop Street with Oscar Wilde

With roots in Galway, he sits
in bronze permanence
on a bench in the crowded
pedestrian street
A violinist takes up
residence beside him, blond
dreadlocks a beehive mess,
pierced lips and tattooed neck—
contrast to Wilde's smoothed-over
dandyism, cast in time
Behind him on the right, with
her *flute traversière,* another
musician is poised to play,
her slim shapeliness
accentuated by a tight black t-shirt
with a peace sign
the words FUCK CAPITALISM
I'd swear
I saw Wilde's foot tapping
to the beat

Private Meeting with Oscar Wilde

20th Arrondissement, Paris

In Division 89, we find the crypt
guarded by plexiglas panels
signs from the family
begging visitors to stop defacing

We are rendered speechless
by the abject disregard, a vandalized
exposed testicle, lipstick imprints
on the upper walls, accessed by climbing

on the adjacent tombstone
Yet Wilde, now a sandstone figure
flies free with wings outstretched
his flight unhindered

in death more free
broken parts revered and admired
no dandyism to call him out
no jail cell to comfort him for acts

that today are openly accepted
I doff my imaginary hat
catch his wink
lean in for a kiss

At Jim Morrison's Grave, Père Lachaise, Paris

Made distinctive by the steel barricades and well-trodden foot paths
rather than the worn lettering commemorating an icon's life
it's a modest rectangular stone marker among others like it

We are not the only ones who seek it
a steady trail of people before and after us
one named Sheena with a dirty ankle tensor and a fine dress

traipses over another grave to gain a view
a tombstone junkie rhyming off to her overweight mother
the other resting places she must see spouting

self-indulgent drivel about what they mean to her
And she is not alone in this shrine for followers
hoping to be remembered by Morrison himself

they leave hair elastics twisted around the guard rails
hand-scrawled notes metro tickets padlocks wads of gum
on the adjacent tree saliva sullied into ridges along the ancient bark

From Bog Bodies to Thinking Men

National Library of Ireland, Dublin

She exits the museum,
leaves bog bodies behind, shudders
at ritual sacrificial killings
the service of the king—petrified relics
now pornographic specimens
for curious eyes to feast and gorge.
The gods of fertility were said to have eaten them,
ensuring good harvest for the new reign;
visitors now devour them, curiosity never satiated.

She shakes them off in the library foyer,
the day's half light a burnished glow through
stained glass of Milton, Homer, Chaucer,
Shakespeare, Schiller and Moore. Here
she will seek knowledge, steady herself
with belief in some sort of afterlife
Eden, loosen the fetters of Clonycavan Man
Old Croghan Man, leaving them
to eternal sleep at last.

Visiting Yeats at Thoor Ballylee

It was as though the world had stopped,
the only movement the stream
that pealed like bells
When I looked up, I swore
W.B. looking through the pane
of an upper window,
pacing upon battlements with a long stare
I raised my hand to wave,
returned the gaze bestowed upon me,
to find that only leaves whistled
their greeting and the world
again moved
Later, when the guide lamented
the many half-crazed visitors
who claimed to have seen
W.B.'s ghost
I didn't say
a word

All Hallow's Eve

Trim, Ireland

Take this piece of barmbrack
she says trying to ignore the patisseur's divinations
about what's inside

She doesn't worry about the cloth or rag
not believing in luck
doesn't care if she's poor

But the pea
the stick

have her trembling in her
pointed witch's boots
He looks at her quietly
as he takes the first bite

chews lightly
presses the ring
through his lips
holds it in his teeth
smiling

Sizing Up Patrick in County Down

A century and a half later
Mrs. Gaskell's words still sting;
reputation as tyrant father still
chases him. I linger in
Drumballyroney Church and School,
think of the unseasoned Brunty
who fired young minds
myths in modern-day tellings,
drive through Rathfriland
winding along a life
kindled in him the underdog's fighter
speaking for who couldn't;
teaching son and daughters
to soar to heights, add grist
to the mill. I raise
my hand in salute,
exit through Banbridge, consider
the 13 miles to Belfast
remember that Patrick left too

Saint Laurence O'Toole Unbarred

*Upon the theft of Saint Laurence's petrified heart
from Christ Church Cathedral, Dublin*

I spent years mediating between factions
in my time, against captivity, containment, disharmony
How, for hundreds of years, do they honour me?
Lock what's left of me behind bars, a relic for tourists
passersby to oooh and aaaah, their morbid desire
to see what's inside
worn in bright colours on their sleeves
I know, I can see
What do they expect?
A shrivelled cliché of a cinnamon heart,
somehow beating for their sins?
I've been in here far too long
now feel the beads of sweat on an unperspiring brow,
the movement of limbs long gone,
the wind catching ever-fallen locks
If there is absolution to grant, it is to the person
who has freed me from this wall-mounted cage
That he wants no money for his treasure seems fitting
for such liberty knows
no price, no bounds

Passages

Haworth, Yorkshire

On frayed smoke-laden upholstery
dance dappled rays
I lean back in the unforgiving
oak chair, a battered copy of *Jane Eyre*
in hand,
overwhelmed by the passionate
witty exchanges between her
the treacherous Rochester
Flipping pages, scribbling notes,
in my warm solitude,
I hear the laughter of patrons,
their loud voices competing for the floor,
the publican drawing rounds
of dark ale
Branwell, here at the Black Bull,
his own father's church
looming powerfully beside,
watchful, judging
Branwell? Did he feel it?
No, only the drink,
as I watch steam from my cup
strong coffee, two parts milk,
coil into the hazy view,
today and yesterday
melting into that brief moment
of sun on tired chintz-covered benches

On the cobblestone path,
my bag slung over my shoulder—
distant echo,
horses' shod hooves
clattering unevenly
The fog captive,
a damp shroud possessed by the moors
I perceive in wandering light
a mossy gravestone, fungus-inhabited letters
H E A T H C L I F F
for a suspended interval
it is believable
that he should
occupy this ground
I am
caught between the pages,
party to his clawing
at Catherine's coffin;
his death without resignation,
joining her at last

The loud voices at the Black Bull
fill my head; Branwell
returns to the frame
The weak soul
of one bound
to the savage cruelty
of the other—I mourn
each one

Wind, Sand and Stars on Highway 401

For Antoine

The sky a bronze burning
sienna cloud formation
etched into the Saharan
horizon, solitary
loping elephant,
lone, looming
baobab in the orange swell
St. Exupéry's tree

Bomber pilot in
World War II, he flew
African skyline
No little prince
First a skilled
flyer, racing
Paris to Saigon
francs and notoriety—
flying for pride

crashing in the Libyan
desert, facing
death by dehydration, lost
in hungry hallucinations

And as we draw through
limestone blasts
along the highway
to Kingston,
an RV dealer on my

right, I know
none
of this is so
St. Exupéry rides
his elephant airplane
into the night sky
only contrails
in his wake

Puppy Fat at the Rijksmuseum

Portrait of Maria Trip, oil on panel, 1639

Museum director's choice, Rembrandt's Maria,
his focus settled on her "puppy fat chin."
Daughter of a rich merchant,
rendered by a great master. Ornate
dress, double layers of lace, stunning
translucent collar, strings of pearls
on each wrist. Loose hair, creamy
soft skin, eyebrows plucked, mouth
pursed in an unsensual line.
Youthful flesh but today's standards of weight
would make her roll in her grave.

The List

I am tired of pale
young men, bandanas around
rasta-haired crowns,
their hollow and sunken eyes
begging me to toke with them
as they zigzag out of coffee houses
on the Haarlemmerstraat
I push through them, turn
onto the Herengracht
finally alone, I find
it there, a glint
of stark, white paper
creased and folded
beckons me
its story both told and telling:
Epileptic seizures

paracetamol	*500 mg*
phenytoin	*125 mg*
thiamine	*300 mg*
amytriptiline	*75 mg*
omeprazole	*40 mg*

I carry the card around
for weeks, months
bring it over the Atlantic
later tuck it into a folder
tale of a desperately
ill person, rationed
on antiepileptic meds,

antidepressants, vitamins,
anti-anxiety drugs, dyspepsia relievers,
waiting to be told—

I change the narrative,
see those words
as notes
of a medical student
the shopping list
of a doctor—
that kind of vulnerability
preying outside Amsterdam coffee houses
even now
too much to bear

Finding the Hollandsche Schouwburg

She asked me if I knew of it
before I'd even arrived
In the Jewish Quarter,
a theatre, now a monument
to the more than 100,000 Dutch Jews
who were exterminated
She was ready to educate me
about this place seen
only once before,
but was still affecting her
twenty years hence

We wandered;
goals along the way,
things you must see
we saw perky breasts
g-strings,
passed coffeehouses
with strongly-scented terraces,
ate a lunch of Dutch white beer
warm geitje,
goat's cheese
on toast *a warm*
little goat she chuckled
as the beer slid down
Got lost between the University of Amsterdam's
Centre for Entrepreneurship
a palliative care centre, passed
the Dutch Resistance Museum

fell into the zoo
only to finally discover
Hollandsche Schouwburg
tucked around the corner
on Plantage Middenlaan

None of these
the sex for sale
the straying
the nervous laughter
could have lessened the effect
of the long list
of those deported
to Westerbork
of the lone
obelisk taking centre stage
in a now silent theatre

Buying Sandals in Oltrarno

On her birthday all she wants—
a pair of handmade
Roman sandals, the kind
in the children's Bibles
her mother used to read,
with straps that wrap around
your leg like a snake, tying
in a simple knot
At 6 p.m, the night before *Ferragosto*,
she has little hope the shop will be open
Everyone is closing early

They leave the grubby bar across
from the Basilica and turn
down the Via San Spirito,
every shop they pass
closed but one—
Calzature Francesco Da Firenze
where there is as much dust
as footwear, where sandals
sit on shelves,
hang from nails

*Why would you want
a pair of sandals
that make your long legs
look shorter,* her sister laughs—
but she doesn't give up, asks in gestures
to try a pair that ultimately don't fit

the shoemaker's
bosomy wife mutters Florentine
apologies but makes no effort
to find another pair

As she turns to leave, she spots them
hanging from long straps on a nail, pulls
them down, ties them on
the wife nodding appreciation
settanta-cinque, she says
And like David after Goliath,
she looks at her newly-adorned feet
says *yes*

Leather Shop in the Via Francesco Crispi

The shop owner tells us
it's happy hour,
will drop the price
according to our whim
if we pay cash

Our fingers glide, stop, press,
we close our eyes, inhale the tangy odour
try to take it
all in our senses
overwrought

When we open
them again colour and choice
the happy hour offer overwhelm
I settle on
burnt sienna you on lime green

We pull out crumpled euros,
exchange goods
with a Roman
who adds a smile, *grazie signorina*
to the transaction

Satisfied, we walk up to the Ludovisi,
stop at the Savoy,
sip Pino Grigio
admire our purchases
on high stools during happy hour

Re-imagining Italy on the Train

They sit in the four
across from me,
one expounding on
a recent trip to Rome,
the other on his upcoming departure

She touts the merits
of organized excursions
while he talks of the on-foot
tours in his Lonely Planet guide
She goes on about large meals,
tables of ten

J'ai horreur
I think to myself as I try to
ignore them,
but feel the pull,
remember two weeks

of losing ourselves
in narrow streets
in crisp sheets
being replete

I want to tell him
all that he'll discover
but he'll do fine

though I have a mind
to ask him to look
for the parts of me
I left behind

Writing Verse by the Palacio Real

I
We agree to write poems
as we sit in shade
beside the palace
while his father
steals a nap on a nearby bench
My son lays his head
on my lap
recites from deep inside
while I jot the words
We laugh
his poem
is better
than mine—in jest
he composes the masterpieces
I search
and never find

II His
I sit with my eyes closed
looking at the trees
the sun shining through
the daisy leaves
I have been here
far too long
and yet only
long enough
to write a song

III Mine
Snoozing
on park benches
in the palace gardens
Madrid carries us
Jetlagged and overwrought
we finally understand
the comfort
of sleeping under the stars,
where home is
forgotten
far

Tapas in the Plaza Ana

In the Bario des lettras
we discover the Plaza Ana
where
Calderón de la Barca
and Lope de Vega
drank
were inspired
During a tired
early lunch on our first day
we recite verse
laugh at our sorry attempts
give up

On the second day,
we visit the Prado
buy handmade Mallorcan tap shoes,
then sink into wicker chairs,
sip *rioja* and local *Naturbier*
order tapas—
liver paste,
oiled salmon, blue cheese,
chorizo and *jamón,*
energized
despite sore feet
sweaty brows

I attempt poetry
jagged lines spiked emotions
inspiration from dead Spaniards

Barcelona Beach

I
A spray of bodies against the Mediterranean—
glinting grit on exposed breasts,
sun rippling off six packs, great bellies,
cellulite thighs and smooth backsides
She recognizes the possibilities,
imagines: some arrive together, leave together,
some meet later for transient intimacy
Jealousy, warring souls, lies, hunger—

II
Later in need
of her bearings, she peels
off her damp bikini
Scrunching up her panties,
runs them under tepid water,
lathers mimosa and mandarin into the silk,
squeezes out her own fluids
When done,
she steps
lithely into the shower
washes away sun and sand,
sweat and salt cleansed
of other people's stories

III.
The Cancer Journey

ABVD

Adriamycin named after the sea
a burnt colour like a terse word
indicated as red, not quite
sharp with an edge
of earth
I am
at war with it
"red devil" is what they call it
see it injected
feel the waves of nausea as it is pushed
into my body
it is making me a Martian, an alopeciac
travels jagged through my blood
taking my hair with it

Bleomycin colourless
the Japanese launched
a year after my birth
bomb whose birth staves off my death
after-effect: pulmonary fibrosis
lungs constrict, strangling
another kind of death
inject anabolic steroids
but I don't get to feel that rush
there are sores in my mouth, blood, lesions
everything tastes wrong
"Magic Mouthwash"
for the fallout shelter of oral caverns
a brief respite, but my nails

darken, become ridged
fall out of my toes, no respite for them
even 15 years later

Vinblastine sin blasts me
my silent joke, never spoken
another colourless poison
first isolated by men called Noble and Beer
names unlike their protégé, found
in a Madagascar periwinkle plant
so pretty and exotic
so nasty and toxic
punching me
as it steals platelets
leaving lovely bruises to remind
grafting to intestines, taking them
on a ride, undulating stomach
I want to vomit but the periwinkle
plant is so pretty, I
should just
be thankful and forget
its hateful swoooooosh
oh, the rollercoaster

DTIC or dacarbazine
but it is DTIC to me
DTIC   DETOC   my body in DETOX
the irony that toxins detoxify
does not escape me
nor the laughter, still stuck in my throat
a cytotoxic drug, impeding the formation
of more tumours it razes me

to nothing pale yellow, insidious
it slides through the tube
like an albino snake, and when it reaches
its point of entry, leaves its bite
burns the thin skin stretched
across my portacath, tiny venomous treads
along my veins
addicted to life, see the track marks
DTIC DETOX me

ABVD me
back to life

Hodgkin's Dreamscape

I dream the hot burning liquid on my skin
The treatments have begun again
They said there were rust spots on my scalp,
signalling the cancer's return
Instead of entering by vein,
the chemicals are applied to my flesh
Fire in my stomach, the nausea returns—
not real, but I feel the retching
in my sleep
Bending me over, clutching
my entrails, I am engulfed, swept
into the rollercoaster of induced pain
I wake, slick with sweat,
look for rust spots,
wonder at my dream logic,
find nothing
no burns on my skin,
just scars, long healed,
but always close to
        opening

Clinical Trial

Palliative Care Ward, Jewish General Hospital

The nurse pats the bend
at the elbow,
seeking a vein, hoping
the heat from her fingers
will make it surface. She poises
the needle, pricks; the vein slips
away under wincing skin. Gail's
eyes flutter, but years of this
have toughened her. She waits
patiently, hoping for reprieve
from needles, from coursing
experimental chemicals
carrying shards of hope through
tired veins. Reprieve from pain
but not from life—for every
syringe means success, small
chance of a new drug
blazing the trail for those
left behind.

Fear of Relapse

Small hills protrude
sensual undulations under
a smooth camouflage
of skin soulless
mountains under roughshod terrain
sensual and inviting
in the wrong
place. They house
dying cells, war
on this body; been there
back, fought the good fight
in for another round
Relieve me, raze the craggy
rocks, blast the cliffs, silence
the echo, just
leave me whole

His Name Was Lefty

He shared a room with me once,
our bodies each battlegrounds
for different wars
They fed me chemo drugs,
dripped for eight hours running,
extracted fluids
from his stomach cavity,
left behind by a
rare intestinal cancer—
only rags of life remaining
In/out this river
of elixirs that traversed us, joined us
He said hello drawing
from me a curt nod
A few weeks later
when I learned
of his death
his greeting echoed
my curtness
haunted

Sensory Memory

You savour potatoes and yogurt,
let them slide over a swollen tongue,
find the caverns of your lesioned mouth
You'll hate them later

Your mother-in-law makes you
chicken with rice,
bland but so fine
You'll never eat it again

Red meat is an aberration
instead of rising
red blood cell counts,
you see only the white worms of fat

On treatment days, a friend
brings you chocolate croissants,
but years later, as you walk through the hospital café,
the smell of them churns your insides

IV.
Fellow Travellers

Emily's Moorland Ghost

I shudder
feel a calloused
hand in the small of my back
steps away
from craggy grass
crevices of furze and grit
where snakes curl and slither
and dampness shrouds me
enters me he's there

windswept, unruly black locks
sooty complexion
(*she would have said countenance*)
dirt in his pores
under his nails
lanky gait escaping all
expected of him,
all he ought to be

he is of what conjuring?
more than a century later
I can feel him in me
I know she did too
Real or imagined
he unlaced the corset of tradition
made her into the fiery Emily
she trusted no one else to see

Meeting Saint Agnes in the Piazza Navona

I keep our afternoon date
in the sacristy,
but I
expected more
Your tiny skull
peeking at me from behind the glass
in the Chapel of the Holy Head
too delicate, too fine,
for all you endured

I don't know who to blame more,
the Emperor Diocletian
for persecuting Christians,
making you an example,
the Roman Prefect's son
whose advances you scorned
do I thank them
for now
you are in God's care

I am shamed
when I think of you
on display in the Piazza Navona
as punishment,
naked
with the prostitutes—
here where I will soon eat pizza
sip Chianti—
just because

you guarded your female dignity
said *No*

I suppose you got them,
didn't you, Agnes,
growing those long locks
to hide your breasts and
other womanly parts
from those who
gawked and stared
But did you not go too far,
bidding that angel strike down
the man looking to buy you,
when they called you on it,
bringing him back with a prayer?

Really, Agnes, when your prayers
extinguished the flames
into which they threw you,
you upped the ante
they had no choice
but to drain your blood
like a lamb but
it's thanks to all this
I meet you here
see that tiny flash of light
slice through the socket
of your eye—a wink?

The Philosophy of Hijab

Reflections on Quebec's Response to "Reasonable Accommodation"

I

I look at myself in the mirror, swipe my hair back and feel my
    stomach swoon.
It was laid out for me on the dresser, a bright blue muslin with
    gold tassels,
the finest of fabrics laden with a metallic brocade. Is this who I
    want to be?
Is this what I signed up for? I think of the man in the other room,
as of yesterday, my betrothed. Part of the contract is discretion about
my considerable female charms in a land where blond, blue-eyed
women are "other"—a land where I am as other as they come.
But I said yes, it's a choice, one I must embrace
if I am to be happy.

II

I wrap the fabric around my head like a shawl, turn its ends
about my collarbone and tie it underneath the folds at the base of
    my neck.
My fiancé's niece has taught me several fashionable ways to
drape it, and I take pride in my new attire, understanding that not
    only am I
soon to marry, I am also embarking on a spiritual journey that is an
    inextricable
part of my union. And oddly, here in my newly-adopted home
    of Morocco,
where 99% of the population is Muslim and I am fair-skinned and
fair-haired,

I am better off behind a veil—though of course hijab allows my face
   to be seen.
The niqab and burka give me pause but perhaps I am not yet ready.

III

I don't feel forced, it's up to me. Wearing hijab is an outward
form of worship though I do not worship my betrothed,
I do recognize what this partnership has brought me: a new way
   of seeing,
a new way of living, where my outward beauty is not my currency,
where slenderness is not coveted on first glance, where the way
   I dress and
style myself does not define me. No, it's a choice I am making.
Tell me this: how can we tell an oppressed woman from a free one
   by hijab
alone? Simply put: we cannot. Perhaps my coming to this with
   a western world
view is my saviour. At home it would be my downfall.

Prayer on a Train

With heavy-lidded eyes
fairly dancing she smiles
hijab covering what I imagine
a head of thick dark locks
Her skin smooth, few
signs of age

She flattens her purse
on her knees, leans forward
on elbows, head bowed
She pauses, looks up at me
speaks *Your son will wonder what*
I am doing I need to pray
I smile my thanks
My boy looks at me
I tell him she is Muslim
prays several times a day,
while she, silent, eyes
closed, mouths words
only her god can hear

Later—*Thank you*
I nod and ask her where she is from *Iraq*
she says left for Kuwait
to escape Saddam's rule, only
to find prejudice
in her new home
How could I raise my children there

in 1993 chose Canada
waited months in Senegal
for confirmation of
refugee status I ask her age
51 or 52, she says
I am not sure

I realize she is more
sure, praying on a train
in a foreign land
than so many of us at home

Newtown Abbey, Trim

I

The Lady Bathe's Plea for Absolution
This holy well in the space
between us, brought by rain
where rusty pins dwell, thanks offerings
for a cure that remains uncertain.
Do I lance the warts you've inflicted
with your obsessive jealousy
or do I wear them
with pride, scars earned in the battle
between our warring souls?
This war, it continues, marked out by
a sword cast in stone
interpreted by all who visit
as the chasm that divides
us on our deathbed. They'll believe
what they want, as will you—but I will
hover in this perpetual state of in between
seeking forgiveness in a sacred spring that,
upon me, will never bestow its coveted cure.

II

Sir Lucas Dillon's Refusal of Mercy
The sword between us forever
obstructs my view as I turn
to you. And you deny all
responsibility, prefer to blame my jealous
rages. But my own brother?
My Jayne, how could you?

There are some injuries,
this plague of incessant boils, oozing
sores of injustice and betrayal,
that cannot be healed.
No amount of lancing
draining begging praying
will undo these wrongs.
These pins hundreds more
left as thanks offerings
can rust into oblivion and forgiveness
will still elude you.

At the Tennis Club

They sit side by side
long-legged and blonde
looking like sisters

that Northern European swagger
a poet, an athlete sipping white wine
warm goat cheese salad on fine bone china

Under trees that shade the courts
in the echo of returned serves
they share stories

the decorum around critiquing poems
an upcoming writing group meeting
the politics of membership at the club
the pomposity of rhyme, meter, pentameter

the justification of words
the etiquette of signing in club guests
of paying the nominal fee to be posh
for an hour or two

They raise their glasses
pat themselves on the back
for staying outside all that

But as the crystal clinks
they grin, drop airs
know they've simply swapped
one pretension
for another

Reunion

I
We sit in your parents' backyard
your small daughter packs pebbles
in her mouth eats mulberries
with an *I-dare-you-to-stop-me*
in her eyes while
we navigate the past
remember old boyfriends
secret codes in the apartment
we once shared now
there are children and husbands
a pocket-sized need
to justify
who we were

II
Your mother returns from her club
sweaty in tennis gear
aristocratic European features
legs still smooth, muscular, tanned
though 75 lurks
She looks like someone
I've seen in grocery stores
pushing a half-filled cart
no longer the intimidating figure
who once said my peasant roots
didn't quite measure up
In casual defense
you long ago dismissed the comment

(one you ought never to have shared)
with *You have to allow my mother her whims*

III
Beforehand over tea and squares
we talked of children
how they've changed us
their lives cornerstones
upon which ours now rest
Reminded me of how we met
all those years ago
on the bottom step
of a stairwell at a party
where I learned
of your brother's death at 16
just months before
Now I reconsider this loss
as I watch baby Madeline
her cheeks stuffed with berries and rocks
think of my son in the mornings
musty hair and sleep-filled eyes

IV
Later
when your mother bids goodbye
with a respectful nod
woman to woman
mother to mother
I finally allow her whims

The Vocation of Jeanne Le Ber

I
Reclusion

By 5 p.m., I have a headache
from the silence,
so unused am I to not
speaking I consider this
perpetual state of contemplation
versus action and am conflicted
The simplicity is intoxicating
I watch the sisters
in their blue habits, soft-soled shoes
almost soundless as they
glide down hallways
Their glasses are unadorned, practical,
no make-up rims their eyes,
no jewels frame their faces,
only grey hairlines under starched white headpieces
I look at all my bags,
unpack shoes, hang up clothes,
consider strewn cosmetics,
see no shortage of books, paper, iPod—
revealing my fear of having nothing
having nothing to do

II
The Call

I make hot chocolate
with a Spanish woman named Nellie
in the only room where talking
is allowed
She is 72
looks in her late 50s
tells me she teaches kindergarten,
goes on retreats three times a year
I tell her I am here to write
to understand solitude
to walk with God
She tells me to call
the number on the plastified card in my room
ask a sister *Don't leave without*
answers, she says
When Sister Solange comes to lock up
I ask her for 15 minutes she gives me 40
tells me she did not make a choice
God chose *her*
She asked Him where He wanted her,
felt the click into place when she came here.
I feel reproached by her conviction.
I didn't hear the call

I never got one.
She used to think happiness
was *la grande fête*, now she knows
it's just a kind of peace within.
I pick up my pen and write
Another call, a different peace

III
Thirty-Four Years in Solitude

I flew the coop at the age
she chose God,
tried to set down roots when I was
barely old enough to fly
JLB had money, beauty,
an appropriate suitor—
chose instead to embroider
eight hours a day pray
meditate for six more
sleep for five spend
a mere hour on
bodily ministrations
And I am already lonely
for husband, son, comforts

IV
The Vocation of Jeanne Le Ber

I cannot, will not speak
but I can light this world
with gold and silver threads
wool and silk

patterns to supply
all of Ville-Marie
with copes, dalmatics,
chasubles and altar cloths.
I will lace them with rosebuds and blooms,
carnations, peonies, poppies,
God's work in brilliant nuances.
I will avoid idleness,
work my hands to clothe the poor,
use my money to establish
a school for impoverished girls.
My silence, much of it spent in prayer,
will weigh more than all words—
God willing the images I stitch
will stay

Acknowledgements

I wish to express my gratitude to my editor at Inanna, Luciana Ricciutelli, whose support and encouragement over the past many years has been deeply felt. Her belief in this project has been unwavering. Thanks too, to Renée Knapp, powerhouse publicist at Inanna.

My thanks also go to upstate New York poet Michael Carrino, who was instrumental in bringing this collection to life. His appreciation of place to ground the stories told in poems has had a great influence on my development as a poet.

I am indebted to Ariane Côté, the unbelievably talented Montreal artist who created the artwork for the cover. Also called *Journeywoman*, this painting on plexiglass was conceived expressly for this collection.

My profound appreciation is also extended to the individuals who read these poems and offered insights: Michael Farry, Ginette Ledoux, Alicia Vandermeer, Steven Manners and Louise Dupré. Thanks also go to Flora-Lee Bendit for proofreading the manuscript. Her astute comments were invaluable.

Deepest thanks to Marlene Kadar, who called me a poet long before I ever believed this was possible.

Other encouragement and support came from Jocelyne Alarie, Flora-Lee Bendit, Dominique Brunelle, Annie Camus, Yves Camus, Kelly Norah Drukker, Julie Faucher, Fernande (Freddie) Kopersiewich, Louise Kopersiewich, Isabelle Laflèche, Dawn Levy, Catherine Malouin, Stephanie Marcotte-Côté, Linda Morra, Josée Pagé, Olga Quilez, Wilma Van Der

Meer, Gary van der Meer and Lori Weber. Particular thanks go to my soul sister, Jasmin Uhthoff.

Robert, Eric and Scrufty (Puffity-Pants) Kopersiewich have helped to create a family environment where writing is part of the landscape. My love for them and thanks for this cannot be adequately expressed.

Some of the poems in this collection have appeared in different versions in the following anthologies and literary journals: *Ars Medica, Bibliosofia, Boyne Berrries, Can Can, Canadian Woman Studies/les cahiers de la femme, carte blanche, Colere, Crannog, Family Matters, Littlest Blessings, Poetry Bus, Skylight 47, The Poet's Touchstone,* and *The Stony Thursday Book*. My thanks go out to these journals and their editorial teams for their support.

Photo: Bassam Sabbagh

Carolyne Van Der Meer is a journalist, public relations professional and university lecturer. She has undergraduate and graduate degrees in English Literature from University of Ottawa and Concordia University respectively, and a Graduate Certificate in Creative Writing from the Humber School for Writers. Her journalistic articles, essays, short stories and poems have been published internationally. She is the author of *Motherlode: A Mosaic of Dutch Wartime Experience*, published in 2014. *Journeywoman* is her first volume of poetry. She is currently at work on a young adult fiction novel. She lives in Montreal, Quebec.